Sight Words

4th Grade Workbook

(Baby Professor Learning Books)

Speedy Publishing LLC
40 E. Main St. #1156
Newark, DE 19711
www.speedypublishing.com

action

the bringing about of an alteration by
force or through a natural agency

action

action

Use it in a sentence.

amount

to reach a total

amount

amount

Use it in a sentence.

chart

information in the form of a table, diagram, etc.

chart

chart

Use it in a sentence.

condition

the state in which something exists;
the physical state of something

condition

condition

Use it in a sentence.

control

to have power over (something)

control

control

Use it in a sentence.

develop

to cause (something) to grow or
become bigger or more advanced

develop

develop

Use it in a sentence.

direct

to cause (someone or something) to turn, move, or point in a particular way

direct

direct

Use it in a sentence.

effect

a change that results when
something is done or happens

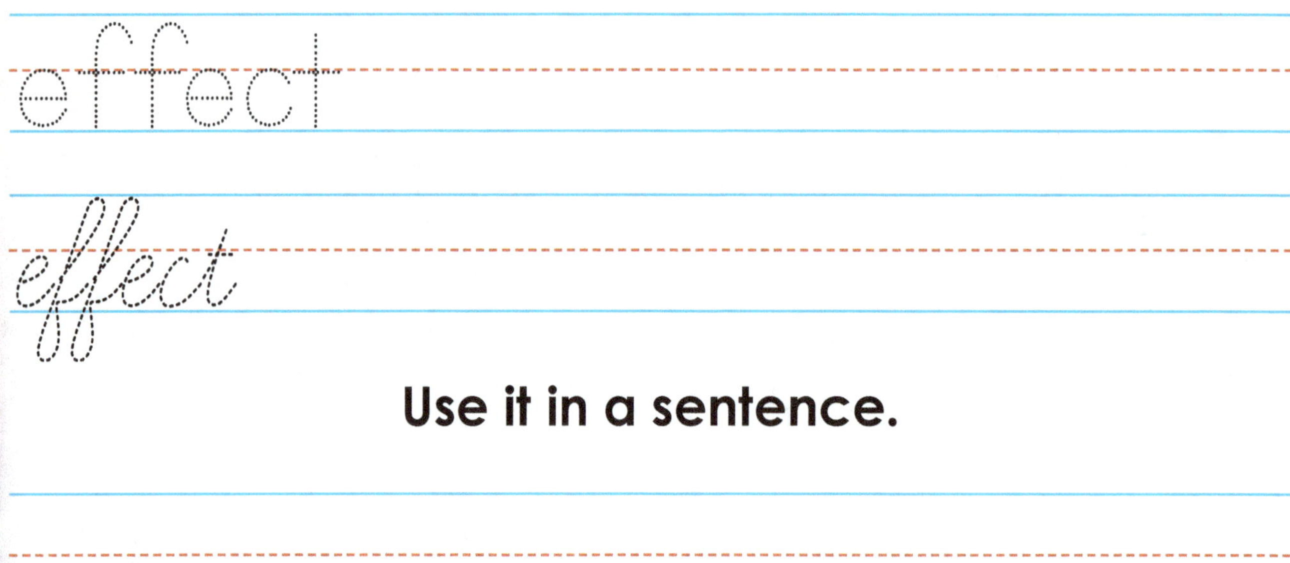

Use it in a sentence.

favorite

a person or a thing that is liked more than others

favorite

favorite

Use it in a sentence.

general

of, relating to, or affecting all the
people or things in a group; involving
or including many or most people

general

general

Use it in a sentence.

history

past events that relate to a particular
subject, place, organization, etc.

history

history

Use it in a sentence.

indicate

to show (something); to show that (something) exists or is true

indicate

indicate

Use it in a sentence.

labor

physical or mental effort

labor

labor

Use it in a sentence.

level

an amount of something

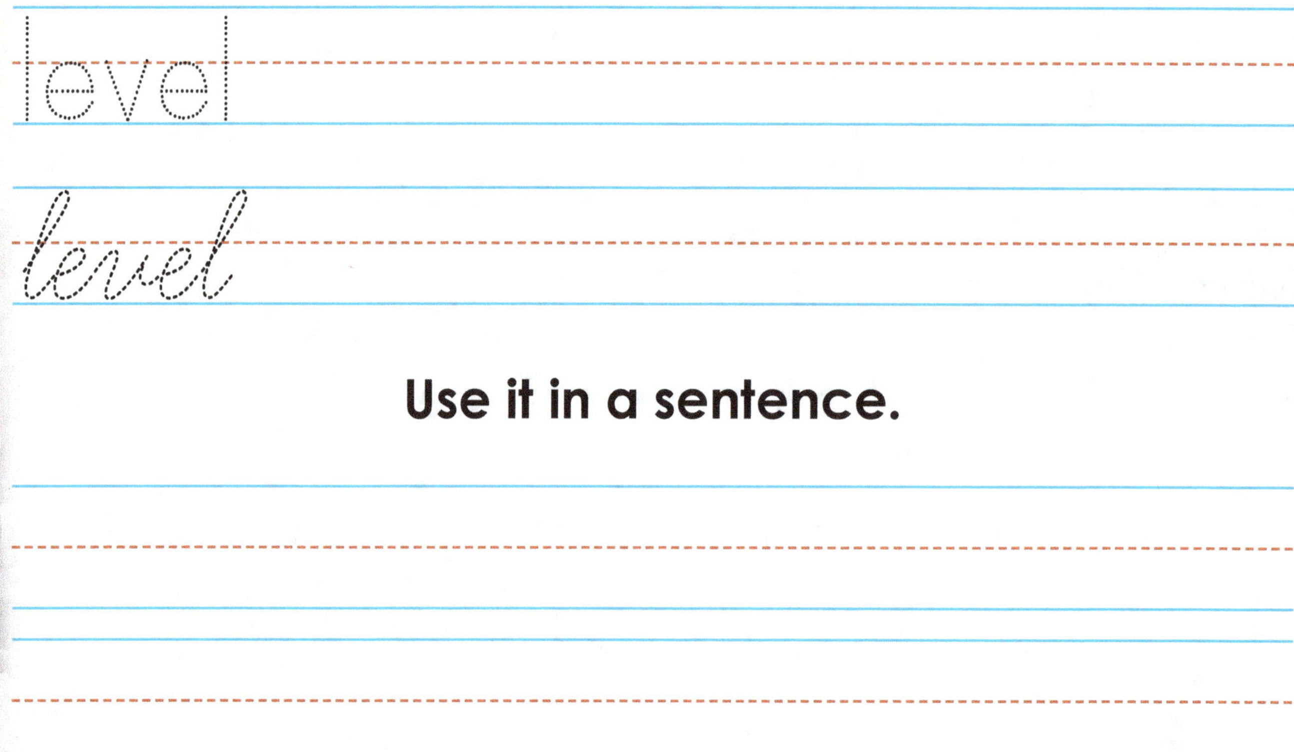

level

level

Use it in a sentence.

measure

an amount or degree of something

measure

measure

Use it in a sentence.

nation

a large area of land that is controlled
by its own government

nation

nation

Use it in a sentence.

opposite

completely different

opposite

opposite

Use it in a sentence.

pattern

a repeated form or design especially
that is used to decorate something

pattern

pattern

Use it in a sentence.

phrase

a group of two or more words that express a single idea but do not usually form a complete sentence

phrase

phrase

Use it in a sentence.

property

something that is owned by a
person, business, etc.

property

property

Use it in a sentence.

replace

to put someone or something new in the place or position of (someone or something)

replace

replace

Use it in a sentence.

rhythm

a regular, repeated pattern of
sounds or movements

rhythm

rhythm

Use it in a sentence.

similar

almost the same as someone or something else

similar

similar

Use it in a sentence.

suffix

a letter or a group of letters that is added to the end of a word to change its meaning or to form a different word

suffix

suffix

Use it in a sentence.

surface

an outside part or layer of something

surface

surface

Use it in a sentence.

total

after everything or everyone is counted

total

total

Use it in a sentence.

tube

a long, hollow object that is used especially to control the flow of a liquid or gas

tube

tube

Use it in a sentence.

various

used to refer to several different or many different things, people, etc.

various

various

Use it in a sentence.

wheat

a kind of grain that is used to make flour for breads, cookies, etc.

wheat

wheat

Use it in a sentence.

Visit

BABY PROFESSOR
EDUCATION KIDS

www.BabyProfessorBooks.com
to download Free Baby Professor eBooks
and view our catalog of new and exciting
Children's Books